GOD

GOD

Answering the Mysteries of God, God's Existence, the Trinity, and God's Love; and How to Have a Personal Relationship with God

James L. Jordan, PhD, PhD

Deovina N. Jordan, PhD, MD

Copyright Page

Copyright © 2019 James L. Jordan, PhD, PhD
and Deovina N. Jordan, PhD, MD
All Rights Reserved.

Title: GOD: Answering the Mysteries of God, God's Existence, the Trinity, and God's Love; and How to Have a Personal Relationship with God

Paperback ISBN-13: 978-1-64752-000-7
E-Book ISBN-13: 978-1-64752-001-4

No portion of this book may be reproduced, scanned, or distributed in any form without the written permission of the authors and Publisher.
Please purchase only authorized editions.

For more information, address:
Deja Jord, Inc.
23811 Washington Avenue, C110 #249
Murrieta, California 92562

Copyright, Legal Notice, and Disclaimer

This publication is protected under the US Copyright Act of 1976 and all other applicable international, federal, state, and local laws, and all rights are reserved, including resale rights.

Although the authors and the Publisher have made every reasonable attempt to achieve complete accuracy of the content in this book, they assume no responsibility for errors or omissions.

If you have any questions about the content of this book, please pray to God and consult the Bible.

Deja Jord, Inc.

Dedication

We dedicate this book to God (Father, Son and Holy Spirit) and to the body of Christ.

James L. Jordan and Deovina N. Jordan

Prologue

This book about God was written to enhance discipleship among true Christian believers, not to entertain them. Bookstores are full of entertaining books, filled with amusing stories, but with little true substance, particularly for those persons who want to learn more about Christian theology. This book represents years of diligent work and authentic Christian living to make it possible. Indeed, it represents about fifty years of the senior author's life to write. As such, it is not structured like the large number of books available in bookstores today. This book was written more along the lines of the historical theological texts of the Christian writings that have endured for centuries and are still exerting an influence in modern times. Examples of such writings still being cited, which did not depend upon stories, include the works of Saint Paul, Saint Peter, Saint Augustine, Saint Thomas Aquinas, Thomas Kempis, Martin Luther, John Calvin, and others. This approach is also in accord with how Biblical scholars in Judaism advanced theology (e.g., large portions of the Torah, Midrash, Babylonian Talmud, and the Jerusalem Talmud). The texts in the aforementioned writings are more about content, not about entertainment value. This is one reason why Jews have endured for two millennia, even while undergoing persecution. Presently, Christianity is the world's most persecuted religion. Christians must adopt such a strategy for Christianity to survive and prosper.

To serve God, one must know God. It is not possible to serve the unknown. The first chapter, titled Who is God and What are His Characteristics?, points out the Biblical truths regarding the Lord God. This is reinforced by the Appendix containing Biblical passages pertaining to God.

The stakes are not only about knowing who God is and about the survival of Christianity, but also in evangelizing non-Christians to Christianity. In that way, the message of God's hope, love, nature, and salvation can reach them also. But, when Christians are weak about their own faith, they cannot effectively fulfill the Great Commission established by Christ. Instead of being able to confidently present their faith, they become weak in doing so. By being weak, they permit science to be used by atheists to deny God, without being able to use science to support Christianity. The second chapter, about order as evidence for the existence of God, refutes arguments used by atheists to deny God's existence.

Christians also permit Muslims to deny the Trinity, saying such is not one God, while not knowing that the Trinity is still only One God. As a consequence, the weakness of Christians works against them regarding Muslims. It also allows for the establishment of Chrislam, an attempt to equally bind the Bible and the Lord God to the Quran and Allah. The consequence is the rejection of the truth of the Bible and the oneness of God. The third chapter, on the oneness of God - solving the mystery of the

Trinity, addresses such arguments. In doing so, the chapter also repudiates polytheism (e.g., Hinduism), alterative paths to salvation (e.g., spiritualism and paganism), and pantheism (the universe is God).

Due to the trend towards conformity and all religions being equal, Christians who follow such teachings permit Buddha (basically an atheist) to become a Messianic figure, thereby diminishing the importance of Christ. Many so-called Christians turn to Mary, when Christians are told to depend solely on Christ for their salvation. The fourth chapter, discussing God - first in love and first in our lives (God in control), addresses the importance of focusing solely upon God, through Christ, for salvation. This message is reinforced by the fifth chapter (opposition to God and the futility of such opposition) and the sixth chapter (getting closer to God). The fifth chapter, as a result, serves to provide support for denying occult practices (e.g., witchcraft, fortune telling, and use of psychic mediums) which are actually acts of rebellion against the Lord God.

Arguments against Christianity are being ineffectively countered by many Christians. By being weak, Christians permit political correctness to define their faith and what they do, even if such means denying part of the Bible and, in particular, the Gospels. When part of the truth is rejected, the result is not the truth, for it becomes blended with other doctrines. Yes, many who profess to be Christians have their humor and their stories, but they become lukewarm in their faith and become separated from God. They sin and they do not know it. As such, they do not repent of their sins. But, they are still judged for their sins. Why? They had the opportunity and the means to become solid in their faith, but they chose the pleasures of being flattered and entertained instead. They chose to be acceptable to the world, but not to God. They have become apostates. As a result, they pay the ultimate price. They do not go to heaven.

Strong Christians are not developed through being entertained while the Word of God is being minimized. And, strong Christians are needed to ensure the survival of the Church. Since the works of the notable theologians of the past are solid, based on a sound foundation, they provided strength for the Christian church to survive hardship. Additionally, their works have endured the test of time and place; they are read across a broad spectrum of humanity. The works of those who only sought to amuse Christian believers and others did not endure the test of time. They are also marginalized from one culture to another. The truth cannot be trivialized. The fact of the matter is that we, the authors, seek to contribute something timeless, independent of place or culture, to theology and not to earn a fortune doing so.

As you will also note, we, the authors, do not write about ourselves. We do not even place our pictures on our works. We seek no acclaim in front of groups. We don't want anything to detract from the message of Christ and salvation through Him and Him alone. We are messengers, not the message.

This book might be boring to some persons. But it might inspire those who seek meat, more than milk, in their Christian faith. Since others are better at storytelling, the book should inspire them and provide them with the means to incorporate the ideas in the book while doing their Christian ministries. The messages within this book will appeal to a segment of the population, but not to all. But, no book appeals to all.

Table of Contents

Chapter One: Who is God and What are His Characteristics?...1

Chapter Two: Order as Evidence for God ……………..9

Chapter Three: The Oneness of God: Solving the "Mystery" of the Trinity…………………………………………………...22

Chapter Four: God: First in Love and First in Our Lives (God in Control)……………………………………………………37

Chapter Five: Opposition to God and the Futility of Such Opposition..48

Chapter Six: Getting Closer to God…………………….53

Appendix: Important Bible Passages Regarding God (King James Version)………………………………………….......58

Chapter One: Who is God and What are His Characteristics?

God is Unique and the Creator

God says that He alone is God, that He is all-powerful, all-knowing, ever-present, eternal, wise, forgiving, and jealous. God is the Creator. He created by His Word. God created all things. He has declared that He is the Creator of the universe, the earth, all life, and mankind. God alone is the Creator.

God also made humanity in His image. He gave both man and woman honor and glory.

Other deities did not create the creation; God did. He did so by His wisdom and His Word. Having established that God is the Creator, the Bible denies that the creation was done by any other deity.

Idolatry (worship of other gods) is forbidden, since only the Lord is God. Graven images are also forbidden; they are vanity (folly).

God and Creation are Different

God is separate from the creation. He created by His Word in a straight forward sequence of creation. There is no other creator and the creation belongs to Him. Besides being the Creator of everything, God sustains His creation.

Not only is the Lord God the Creator, and the creation is sustained by His power, God also has dominion over the creation. He owns the creation and maintains authority over the creation.

Only God is God

God asserts that He alone is God, that there is no other god with Him, and that He is eternal, spirit, and unlike any other. Being eternal and immune to time, God's existence is *a priori* to the creation. Since God is not beholden to time, He does not grow weary.

Not only is God eternal, He is forever blessed. God is flawless, perfect and above all others. God is love who revealed His love towards humanity through His Son, Jesus Christ.

No one judges God. But, God judges all. God makes the laws. His laws are pure, perfect, and wise, for nothing unclean comes from God.

Only the Lord is God. There is no other god. The Father is our God. The Son is our Lord. They are one God. There is a temptation to conceive of the Father and the Son as two distinct Gods. But, the Biblical Lord is only one God.

God is Omnipotent (All-Powerful)

God has power over everything and everyone. No one can resist Him or undo what He does. God's power is incomprehensible for mankind; it is overwhelming and absolute. As God has power and His voice has power, His works are solid. God's ways are eternal and what He does cannot be undone by others. While God's Word and laws are perfect, perfection is attainable only through the Spirit of the Lord.

God is Eternal, Unchanging and Omnipresent (Ever-Present)

God asserts that He is eternal (the first and the last). He has no beginning and no ending. God never changes. He is Lord over time.

God is eternal and is the one through and by which creation ensued. Creation has a beginning, God does not. God is also distinct from the creation.

God is omnipresent; wherever one may go, He is there. There is no escaping or hiding from God's presence. Nothing can be hidden from Him. God's knowledge is without limits. He knows every mankind's thoughts and deeds, and He also reveals secrets. Since God is all powerful and no one can withstand Him, He is the ideal protector.

God is Righteous, Merciful and Sovereign

God is righteous. What He does is righteous. Since God loves righteousness, His judgment is righteous. As God wants to uphold righteousness, He teaches mankind on righteousness.

God is merciful. He is also patient and aware of the limits of mankind. God saves. He redeems. While God's Word and laws are perfect, perfection is attainable only through the Spirit of the Lord.

The Lord God is the only God and He is sovereign over mankind. Every believer acknowledges His Sovereignty and no one can resist Him. Believers proclaim His Lordship. The Lord is a God of glory. His glory is overwhelming and eternal. His name alone is glorious.

God has a People for Himself

God chose a people and blessed them. The people did not choose God; He chose them. God is their king, leader, protector, and teacher. No one is as trustworthy as Him. God is also faithful. He strengthens and blesses His people. Humanity needs to turn to God, trust in Him, and do as He teaches.

God Blesses, Guides, Judges, and Sustains His People

God has the power to bless whomever He prefers. He blesses those who trust in Him. God desires repentance of transgressions and blesses faithfulness.

In addition to blessing His people, God rebukes and subdues those who oppose His people. Therefore, salvation thru God is assured and eternal. But, God will not tolerate rebellion from His people.

As God is also capable of anger, He chastises, rebukes, and punishes. God rejects false worship and sacrifices. He does not need untruthful words and material sacrifices from people. He is in direct opposition to the wicked. Therefore, God is also Judge over everyone and everything.

God's people acknowledge Him; they are His witnesses. Since He has chosen a people as His own, He is also their ruler, leader, and teacher. It is a charge that He never wavers from. God has said that He will neither fail nor forsake His people. Not only has He chosen a people, is their Lord and their teacher, God also sustains and strengthens His people. Indeed, He has indicated that humanity does not live by bread alone, but by every word that proceeds out of His mouth.

Everyone should praise God and give Him thanks. Consequently, mankind should not praise any other deity but follow the one and only trustworthy God. Since the Lord accepts those who seek Him, and blesses these people as well as redeems them, then mankind should base its hope in Him and only Him.

God is Life and is Forgiving

The Lord God not only promises life, but He Himself is the life that is promised. He even ransoms His people from the grave. Being kind, God is forgiving. He has indicated that His thoughts are of peace, not of evil. God desires that mankind repents of its transgressions against Him and His teachings. He shows this by forgiving His people and blessing their obedience. Being forgiving to His people and the only God, the Lord then is the only way to salvation and the only Savior for mankind.

God is Accessible

God listens to the prayers of His faithful people. Being accessible to them, God answers their prayers. He warns that trust in man is iniquity, but trust in Him is rewarded.

God is to be Known

It is critical to know God. And, to know God, one must seek Him. If one seeks God and finds Him, then the faithful will be accepted and blessed. The Scriptures tell its faithful believers to honor God and to accept His corrections. Therefore, faithful believers are to glorify God and keep themselves pure, for they (His children) are the temples of the Holy Spirit.

God is the Only Savior

The Father, Son, and Holy Spirit are one God. He is the only savior. God is not removed from His people. He loves His people so much so that He sent His one and only Son, Jesus Christ, to live among men and save the sinners.

God said He is betrothed to His people in righteousness, judgment, loving kindness, mercies, ... [and] faithfulness. God sustains those who follow Him. In return, He desires faith in them. Trust in God is exhibited by following His teachings and

His ways. As a reward for believing in God and following Him, the Lord gives the faithful eternal life and subdues death forever.

Chapter Two: Order as Evidence for God

Some people have claimed that creation and all that exists can be explained by the laws of physics. But, for the laws of physics to even exist, order must exist. Therein lies a problem (order has to precede laws). Since order does not arise from disorder, then the laws of physics cannot emerge independently. For, to do so, one has to violate a law of physics (thermodynamics) that all things go in the direction of disorder. As such, the order needed for the laws of physics to occur would not simply exist. Moreover, since the laws of physics are logical, logic also has to exist. Logic does not emerge from illogic. Logic is a presentation of the existence of intelligence.

The presence of order and logic occur throughout the scientific world. This chapter will now touch on some of those presentations of order and logic that, if things are based on random chance, should not occur.

Laws of Physics

Physical laws are logical conclusions (stated facts) based upon scientific observation and experimentation. They are called laws because they reflect consistency. Examples of laws in physics include (but are not limited to) Ampere's law, Archimedes principle, Avogadro's law, Beer Lambert law, Bell's theorem, Bernoulli's principle, Biot-Savant law, Boltzmann equation, Boyle's law, Bragg's law, Brewster's laws, Carnot's theorem, Charles' law, Clausius statement, Coulomb's law, Curie-Weiss law, Curie's law, Dalembert's principle, Dirac equation, the Doppler effect, Einstein's mass-energy equation, electric potential due to a point charge, Faraday's law, Faraday's laws of electrolysis, Fick's law of diffusion, Fourier's law, Gauss's law, Graham's law, Helmholtz equation, Helmholtz free energy, Hooke's law, ideal gas law, Joule's laws, Kepler's law, Kevin Maxwell relations, Kirchhoff's law, Kirchhoff's second law, Planck equation/ statement, Hubble's law, Lambert's cosine law, Langrangian point, law of conservation of energy, law of equipartition of energy, laws of reflection, laws of thermodynamics, Mach number, Maxwell's equations, Newton's law of universal gravitation, Newton's three laws of motion, Ohm's law, Pascal's law, Raman scattering, radioactive decay law, Stefan's law, Tyndall effect, the uncertainty principle, wave particle duality, Wiedemann-Franz law, Wien's law, and Zeroth law of thermodynamics. The important thing to note is that there are many laws of physics, each detailing a component of reality that is consistent, observable and reproducible. In other words, the laws of physics represent a high degree of logic and are not the result of simple random chance.

Subatomic and Atomic Consistencies

At the subatomic level, the first generation of the lepton particle, the electron, occurs. An electron is a first generation lepton subatomic particle with a mass of 9.10938356(11) × 10^{-31} kg (or 5.48579909070(16) × 10^{-4} u) and an electric charge of -1 e (−1.6021766208 (98) × 10^{-19} C or −4.80320451 (10) × 10^{-10} esu). If the electron resulted from randomness, the consistency of the electron mass and the electric charge would vary. But, there are no partial electrons or electrons that are more than the single electron noted (e.g., an electron 1.5 times larger than the other electrons).

The proton is a subatomic particle primarily composed of 2 up quarks (u) and 1 down quark (d). A proton has an electric charge of +1 e (1.6021766208(98) × 10^{-19} C). The mass of a proton is 1.672621898(21) × 10^{-27} kg (or 1.007276466879(91) u). If the proton resulted from randomness, the consistency of the proton mass and the electric charge would vary. Like the electron, there are no partial protons such as only up quarks, or only down quarks, or only one up quark and one down quark. There are no super protons such as three (or more) up quarks or two (or more) down quarks. The composition of protons is consistent.

The neutron is a subatomic particle primarily composed of 1 up quark and 2 down quarks. A neutron has mass of 1.674927471(21) × 10^{-27} kg (1.00866491588(49) u) and an electric charge of 0 e. If the neutron resulted from randomness, the consistency of the neutron mass and the electric charge would vary. Like the proton, the there are no partial neutrons such as only up quarks, down quarks, or one up and one down quarks. There are no super neutrons such as two (or more) up quarks or three (or more) down quarks. The composition of neutrons is consistent.

Electrons, protons, and neutrons are consistent in the manner in which they form atoms. The consistency of atomic structure permits categorization into specific elements that have been arranged in a periodic (elemental) chart. Each element has its own characteristics such as atomic number, electron configuration, and recurring chemical properties. Such would be highly unlikely if order was the consequence of randomness and chaos. Instead, the periodic chart shows not only order, but also logic.

Water

Water is unique among the chemicals. It is most dense above its freezing point and floats upon liquid water when it freezes. If that were not the case, then water in its solid (frozen) form would sink. Oddly enough, hot water freezes faster than cold water (discovered first by Aristotle). Water exists in a liquid state. And, a liquid state is a necessity for the development and sustainment of life. If everything is the result of random occurrences, then why is the only exception (that of water being unique) the very one that permits life?

Biochemical Compounds

A vast variety and complexity of molecules are involved in life. Notable among these are amino acids, proteins, sugars (e.g., monosaccharides), nucleic acids, and lipids. The 22 proteinogenic amino acids (20 of which are encoded in the genetic code) are all L-stereoisomers, meaning that they exhibit spatial isomerism. In other words, the molecular formula and constitution (sequence of bonded atoms) are the same as D-stereoisomers, but they differ in three-dimensional space regarding the orientations of their atoms. While some D-isomers are utilized in bacterial envelopes, as a neuromodulator (D-serine), and in some antibiotics, amino acids used in living organisms have L-stereoisometry, meaning that the D-isomers are basically useless regarding protein structure. If amino acids were used randomly, then stereoisometry would be irrelevant. But, that is not the case. Stereoisometry of amino acids is an important factor in life.

In contrast to amino acids being L-stereoisomers, all naturally occurring monosaccharides (e.g., galactose, glyceraldehyde, glucose) are D-isomers. As noted with amino acids, such would not occur if sugars were utilized at random (since sugars at random would be half D-isomers and half L-isomers). But, randomness in the utilization of monosaccharides does not occur. Thereby, order is involved in both the selection and utilization of both amino acids and of monosaccharides.

Biochemical Pathways

Biochemical pathways involve metabolites (reactants, products, intermediates) in sequential, ordered series of reactions catalyzed by enzymes and are located (in eukaryotic cells) in different locations of the cell. The enzymes themselves are produced by pathways linked to inherited information associated with pathways and specific enzymes (also produced by biochemical pathways). The information for the formation of enzymes is communicated by pathways, linked to the genetic code, and specific enzymes. As such, an extremely linked, complicated, and yet logical, ordered system emerges. Breaks in the pathways or links among pathways lead to disease, failure to communicate needed information for pathways to exist, and/or the inability for life to exist. That order is absolutely necessary for life to even exist. Life cannot exist at random; even synthesis of organic molecules does not yield life. Organic molecule synthesis, outside of life, tends to be of very simple molecules when left to chance. More complicated organic molecules require intelligence (e.g., human) to synthesize outside of living organisms. In order for life to exist, life must perpetuate itself using substrates and biochemical pathways in a consistent and interconnected manner. The resulting biochemical pathways (e.g., in human cells) are very complex with many intersecting pathways. The necessary complexity and intersectionality requires a very high level of order and logic.

    The order of biochemical pathways is reflected in a number of metabolic pathways (many of which also involve feedback inhibition). Included are glycolysis, the Krebs' (citric acid) cycle, fatty acid β-oxidation, gluconeogenesis, oxidative phosphorylation, pentose phosphate pathway, and urea cycle. The complexity of metabolic pathways can be demonstrated by addressing just a few pathways. Glycolysis (which reduces glucose into pyruvate) involves ten reactions, ten enzymes, and adenosine triphosphate. Glycolysis occurs in the cytosol. Gluconeogenesis (which results in glucose being generated from specific non-carbohydrate substrates) involves glycogenic amino acids and eleven enzyme-catalyzed reactions. Gluconeogenesis commonly occurs in the liver. Oxidative phosphorylation (which leads to release of energy to produce adenosine triphosphate [ATP]) not only involves metabolites and enzymes, but also the oxidation of the reduced form of nicotinamide adenine dinucleotide [NADH]). Gluconeogenesis occurs in the mitochondria. Note that each of the mentioned biochemical pathways is sequential; involve specific metabolites and enzymes, and different biological regions. Thus, biochemical (metabolic) pathways are a demonstration of order and logic. They are not collections of randomly occurring chemical reactions.

If a slight alteration exists in a protein (e.g., enzyme), for example, such as the substitution of a single amino acid for another among many amino acids in that protein, the protein's function is altered. The resulting protein can become nonfunctional since its structure has changed. Many genetic diseases (e.g., sickle cell disease) result from the change of a single amino acid in the protein. Such a change can also be incompatible with life. But, at random, proteins associated with genetic mutations (e.g., with altered amino acid composition/order) should be much more common than they actually are. After all, if two amino acids appear closely related, then changed by a mutation at random, they would appear at random/intermixed (without ordered structure or function). The altered protein, in the case of an enzyme, would also lose its biochemical properties as a catalyst. That is because other amino acids, not currently present in natural systems, should be present and also impact the formation, structure and properties of enzymes and other proteins. But, order is the norm, not the exception.

Genetic Code

Thousands of genes are necessary to create an organism. Humans have between 20,000 and 30,000 genes. Tomatoes have more than 30,000 genes. The genes represent nucleotide triplets of deoxyribonucleic acid (DNA) and ribonucleic acid (RNA) that contain the genetic information of living cells. Being information (in a chemical format), the genetic code thus comprises rules (a consistent format) to translate information from nucleic acids into proteins. The proteins thereupon carry out processes necessary for life to exist. The genetic code has been compared to computer code necessary for a computer to function. But, the genetic code is even more sophisticated than the computer code. Computer code is based on a binary system, but the genetic code contains nucleotide triplets. Like the repeating pattern of a binary system, the nucleotide triplets code for specific amino acids. But, one catch (requisite) for the genetic code to operate is that the presence of proteins is needed during the conferring of information from the nucleotide triplets to amino acids and ultimately to proteins. In essence, the genetic code, just like the computer code, is based on logic, not upon random happenstance.

Cells, Tissues and Organ Systems

Organ systems are linked. They do not work in isolation as failure of one leads to death of all. Under a random, evolutionary angle, death is the favored condition, not life.

In fact, life depends upon the coexistent functioning of different organelles (for prokaryotes and single cells), tissues comprising organs, and organs comprising systems. For a single cell entity, life can depend upon the mitochondria to produce energy for the cells to function but also on the ribosomes to produce the enzymes needed to produce that energy.

For organs, different tissues are involved in the proper functioning of an organ. For example, the heart needs connective tissues to hold it together and cardiac muscles for it to function. Without either the connective tissues or the cardiac muscles, the heart would not perform properly.

On top of that, organ systems affect each other. The renal system and the cardiovascular system are complexly interdependent. The nervous system and the musculoskeletal system are intricately interconnected. The endocrine system and the reproductive system are closely interrelated. If not so, then the growth, development, and maturation of an individual would not be possible.

The end result is an extremely complicated interaction of cells, tissues, and organs necessary for the functioning of a single higher life form (e.g., a human). The higher life forms, along with the lower life forms (e.g., the bacteria in the human gut necessary for proper digestion), also interact. As such, the scope of complexity regarding life increases considerably.

In spite of all that complexity, there is logic to all of these. One can understand how the different organelles, tissues, and organs function and interact. When one understands the intricacies of it all, one becomes very impressed about how fine-tuned life is, with the remarkable interactions of the different systems, to result in a functioning organism. Such would not arise from random interactions. Random interactions would not produce the symphony of life expressed in the cells, tissues, and organ systems. The close cooperation, communication, and interface of cells, tissues, and organs are more likely the result of logic that emerges from intelligence.

Intelligence

Intelligence is not a common component in the universe. But, life forms exhibit intelligence. How can intelligence, which depends upon some understanding of order, come from the lack of order? On top of that, the brain is extremely complex. The human brain contains about 86 billion neurons which interconnect via synapses. There are over 1,000 trillion synapses in the human brain, about 1,000 times more than the number of stars in the Milky Way galaxy. From those billions of neurons and synapses, the human brain makes about 20 million billion calculations each second. If intelligence could be produced at random, then one would at least expect to find some sort of computer, even a microchip, develop in the natural world. But, there are no computer chips forming in geological/ material sciences. But, the brain, which is far more efficient than a computer chip, does exist.

The Galaxy, Solar System and Earth

Around 700 quintillion planets exist in the universe, but there is only one Earth. Stars are more plentiful than planets, within the approximately 100 billion galaxies in the universe. Those galaxies contain about 10^{18} stars (a billion trillion). But, life does not live on stars. For a star to be able to even support life, its metallic (elements heavier than helium) content must have an appropriate composition. The sun is unusually metal-rich for a star of its size and does have the right metallic composition. This encourages planets to orbit around it. Additionally, in order for a star to sustain life, that star cannot be too close to the center of a galaxy nor can it be part of the spiral arms. The star must be in a Galactic Habitable Zone. Too close to the center of the galaxy, the enormous gravitational combined pull of clustered stars would disrupt the Oort cloud (which surrounds the outer perimeter of the Solar system and contains trillions of comets). If the Oort cloud was perturbed by the gravitational pull of many close stars, many comets in the cloud would be directed at earth with ensuing comet impacts and, consequently, extinguishing life on earth. Moreover, a planet becomes uninhabitable closer to the center of the galaxy as it would be exposed to excessive radiation (e.g., cosmic rays, gamma rays, X-rays). The excessive radiation is not conducive to the existence of life. In addition to the Galactic Habitable Zone being sufficiently distant from the center of the galaxy, for a star to be able to support life, that star must not be exposed to the spiral arms of the galaxy. The intense radiation and gravitational pull of a spiral arm are also not favorable to life. Fortunately, the sun has an orbital period that approximates the pattern speed of the arms, keeping it clear of the spiral arms. This is not normal for other stars of the same age as the sun; their orbits are more elliptical.

The earth's position with respect to the sun is also important in sustaining life. Earth exists in the Goldilocks (habitable) region of a star (the sun) in which the temperature is right for liquid water to exist. The presence of water is not enough (e.g., the moon and Mars have water), it must be liquid for life to exist. Additionally, the moon has an important role in the development of life on earth. Because of its gravitational pull, the moon causes the earth to have a tilt when rotating around the sun. This not only results in the development of the seasons (and, therefore, life), but also in keeping the earth from freezing over (thereby, becoming lifeless).

Life on earth would also not exist if not for the presence of Jupiter. Jupiter serves to catch asteroids which, if allowed to descend on earth, would cause extinction of life on earth. The earth is also protected by its magnetic field that protects its atmosphere from the onslaught of the solar wind and cosmic rays from the universe. The magnetic field deflects the solar wind and cosmic rays so that their paths become twisted and bent. Without an atmosphere, life on earth would not exist. The earth's atmosphere also provides a protection for life. The ozone layer protects life from the sun's harmful ultraviolet radiation. And, the atmosphere itself causes most bodies (e.g., meteorites) to burn up before hitting the planet's surface; thereby, also protecting life. The protections for life on earth due to the location of solar system, earth, the moon, Jupiter, magnetic field, and ozone layer are all occurring simultaneously. The end result has a major implication for life on earth; for life is logical. Consequently, life is able to exist.

Conclusion

Creation (from subatomic and atomic particles; water; biochemical compounds and pathways; genetic code; cells, tissues and organ systems; to the universe) is filled with logic. Logic arises from intelligence. Such intelligence is indicative of a creator. That creator is God.

Chapter Three: The Oneness of God: Solving the "Mystery" of the Trinity

Copyright © 2016, James L. Jordan and Deovina N. Jordan

God is One. There is no other god. Only God is the Lord God. All others who would claim to be gods are false. They are not gods; they are not God.

There can be only One who is omnipresent. Two things cannot occupy the same space; the same is true spiritually. Only One can be everywhere.

There can be only One who is omnipotent. When two or more are powerful, the most powerful overwhelms the less powerful. But, when One is omnipotent, there is no need to overwhelm anyone (any other being) or anything.

There can be only One who is eternal. One was at the onset of everything; One will be there at the end of everything. Even though there may be many who arise from, or who are created by, the One, only the One can be eternal.

To be omniscient, one would also have to be eternal, omnipotent, and omnipresent. Without those three characteristics, one cannot be omniscient. But, only One is eternal, omnipotent, and omnipresent. As such, only One can be omniscient. And, because that One Being is omniscient, He would have no need to change His mind. In fact, considering His complete, infinite, and eternal nature, He would also be immutable (unchangeable).

Mathematically speaking, there can only be one set of numbers that contains all numbers and is infinite. Subsets can be derived that are infinite in character, but they still do not comprise the whole. If interactions in the subsets are permitted, then more than one subset, or person, may comprise the totality and be one set (substance) in the end. The subsets then become interactive, woven together, one substance, even though they are separate entities. This also answers the issue regarding the death of Christ. Since the infinite subsets interact, they can also resurrect (reconstitute or reconstruct) the third subset.

A major point is that the infinite can give rise to the infinite or to the finite (by creating the finite). Even if the infinite creates the finite, the infinite remains intact. In contrast, the finite can only give rise to the finite, but never to the infinite. That which is finite can never become infinite, no matter how much it may expand (mathematically speaking: approaching infinity). For something to expand, it cannot be by definition ever capable of becoming infinite. Something that is infinite cannot become finite, but it can give rise to and contain many finite sets. The infinite, however, can appear to be finite in that it can place limits upon itself (but which no other set can place on it). One way it does this is by limiting the mathematical subsets or functions being considered at a single moment in time. Another way is how it interacts with the finite subsets that it had formed. As such, the infinite can limit what it does so that it operates in the realm of the finite. But, that does not mean that the infinite becomes finite. To indicate that the infinite can become finite is much like saying one can take a shovel and dig a hole in the ocean, expecting the hole to remain a hole. Every time a shovelful of water is removed, a shovelful of water enters the gap and refills it. Every time something is taken from infinity, it refills and remains infinite. Finally, that which is not omnipresent at the onset can never become omnipresent. That which is not omnipotent from the beginning can never be omnipotent at the end.

That the infinite limits itself when interacting with the finite is beneficial to the finite. Why? If the finite was to be exposed to the true overwhelming nature of the infinite and eternal, it would be overwhelmed. The finite would simply cease to exist. So, when God interacts with humanity, He does not show His entire splendor and His complete nature. For if He did so, humanity would perish. That is a major reason why God the Son came to the world as a man (Christ), limited to a flesh (finite) nature during a period of (finite) time, while still retaining His Godhood. To come only as a finite being, God the Son would not be God. But since God the Son is complete, infinite, and eternal, to come without His divine nature, He would have to deny Himself. God would cease to be God. At the same time that God the Son came as part of the Trinitarian God, He also came as completely human (Christ). If he had come unto humanity in His infinite, eternal, and complete spiritual nature, humanity itself would have perished. For flesh is not capable of enduring that which is eternal, much less even come close to understanding the complete glory, power, and holiness that comes with being totally complete. Aside from overwhelming others who are finite, another reason why God the Son, a part of the Trinity and an infinite Being, came in the flesh as Christ was that His finite nature is so important since it permitted Him to take on the penalty of sin to save believers. Without doing so, Christ's sacrifice would have no meaning. Christ's death would have only been a representation of Christ as an infinite Being, but not death as finite beings endure. Moreover, since the infinite cannot perish and become a sacrifice to redeem others, the sacrifice had to come as finite. By having a finite nature, Christ died and experienced the true impact of death and the penalty of sin. That makes salvation possible for believers and makes Him the intercessor, as shall be discussed later, unto the infinite. And, doing so did not abrogate, in any way, His Godhood.

Retaining God the Son's Godhood has a major impact. For access to the infinite has to be done through the infinite. First, if access to the infinite, complete Being of God could be mediated through a finite being, some control would then be exerted over the infinite by the finite. But, that would not be possible. Nothing finite can come even close to placing any parameter around the infinite. Only the infinite can limit itself, including being in the flesh, dying, and resurrecting again unto life. But that does not transform the infinite into a finite. God remains infinite, even when He has shown to have a finite nature. Second, in comparison to the number set that contains all numbers, the infinite is the only incorruptible set and the only set capable of completely correcting error in a finite set. Thus, since God is completely holy (He is completely free from any possibility of corruption or error), only God is capable of forgiving sins and purifying sinners to holiness. Therefore, the infinite God could offer salvation only by and through Himself. That is why Christ claimed that He was the only way to God the Father. And, that only makes sense since God the Son, Christ, is also an infinite, eternal, and complete Being of the Trinitarian God. By being finite (with His finite nature), Christ opened the door to other finite beings to have union with Him. By being infinite (with His infinite nature), Christ is the way by which we have communion with the infinite. That can happen only if one Being, namely Christ (God the Son), has two natures, one being flesh (finite) and the other being God (infinite).

Having an infinite nature, in addition to his finite nature, also brings upon the sinlessness of Christ. While His finite nature was subject to all that which flesh is exposed, His infinite nature was always able to correct any errors in His finite nature even before they happened. For example, Satan could tempt Christ's finite nature, but Satan could never be successful in making Christ's infinite nature to yield. Consequently, Christ had, within His one being, the ability to be self-correcting for error even before the error could even occur. But, as finite persons, without an infinite nature, mankind does not have that self-correcting capacity. As such, without an incorruptible, infinite input, no matter what mankind does, it can never rid itself of errors (or sins). Fortunately, God has provided a solution for that. Christ becomes not only the One to which humanity can bind, He also becomes the way for God to counsel and guide believers, thereby correcting believer's errors. The Holy Spirit, the infinite, incorruptible and complete Being of the Trinitarian God, is also capable of correcting errors in finite beings. As such, although believers do not innately (inherently) have the two nature (finite and infinite character) of Christ, believers do obtain elements of such a dual nature through the Holy Spirit. Unfortunately, while believers are still in the flesh, their finite nature still takes on errors (or sins). God lets believers retain their personhood even when He resides within them. That is for the believers' benefit. For in His wisdom and His love, God does not overpower mankind with His infinite nature, but works in Christian believers so that they are perfected while still keeping their individual identities (personhoods). To permit that process, Christian believers cannot do so through attempts at correcting their errors (e.g., through good works), but by permitting God to do so through having faith in Him. For, Christian believers cannot control what God does, but Christian believers can have faith in what God does.

The work of the Holy Spirit becomes particularly apparent on the resurrection. When Christian believers are resurrected unto a new life, the work of the Holy Spirit within them will be complete. Then, Christian believers will be without error. And, as an added blessing, Christian believers will no longer be subject to committing errors (or sins) again. When Christian believers are resurrected, although they will hold far greater power than anything (besides God) that people worshipped as deities, and even greater power than even the angels (fallen or non-fallen), Christian believers will still not be gods (as God alone remains the only God). And, even though Christian believers will judge even the angels (including Satan), Christian believers will still not be gods (little/ lesser gods). For, at that time, Christian believers will become sons and daughters of God. Christian believers' nature, power, love, and judgment will be in complete agreement with the nature, power, love, and judgment of the One and only God. And, even then, Christian believers will still be persons in their own rights.

    Retaining His Godhood was a functional component in Christ being able to resurrect from the dead and to resume His position in the Trinitarian Godhead. After all, God the Son, also referred to as being the Word, existed for an eternity before dying in the flesh. He was already infinite and complete in nature. Time is not a constraining parameter on Him who can traverse time at will (as an omnipotent Being who is truly eternal would be capable of doing). From a mathematical standpoint, time is merely a subset in a much larger numerical set. As such, God the Son, Christ, was resurrected into an infinite and complete nature. No one other than God can do that. All others had a beginning, but God the Son, Christ, did not. All others were always finite, but God the Son, Christ, was already infinite who took on a finite form to reveal Himself unto the finite. In so doing, Christ became completely human, with human attributes such as emotions and constraints. Yet, He is not the union of two Gods, but still one God and He retained His position in the Trinity.

    The resurrection of God the Son, Christ, was also essential for the Godhead. For, not only was the Word with God the Father from the eternal past, God the Father did all things through the Word and the Word was and is God. Without the Word, God the Father would not do all things as He had done and He would cease to be the immutable God. Without resurrecting God the Son, a Being/ Person of the Trinitarian God, God would have allowed finite beings to place a limit around, manipulate, alter, and terminate His eternal, infinite, and complete nature. But, God did not allow that to happen. As such, God the Son was resurrected and reunited with God the Father and God the Holy Spirit. Moreover, from a mathematical model, death becomes another mathematical function, limit, or restriction. As such, death may exert a permanent influence on something finite, but it would not exercise the same impact on the One Being who is complete, infinite, and eternal. That which is infinite can always overwhelm something which is finite, if that is the intention of the infinite. As such, it is not death that overwhelms the complete, infinite, and eternal Being. Instead, the complete, infinite, and eternal Being overwhelms death. Death becomes merely another mathematical function within a complete and total mathematical/ number set.

The existence of the Trinity has been touched on repeatedly so far in this document. Having addressed the nature of God, the following questions also arise: "How about the Trinity? Can it be One?" Yes, it can. The Trinity is seen as three persons and one substance. It can be analogous to water in the tri-phasic state as water can exist in three forms (solid, liquid, gas). Water has only one substance, but it can exist in three different states. Any one of the three states of water (solid, liquid, gas) can be transformed to any of the other two states of water. Likewise, God the Father is quite capable of resurrecting God the Son from the dead.

The use of water to explain the Trinitarian nature of God has been performed before. However, the explanation used is inherently flawed. The comparison is made to water being in three containers. Since the water in each container is identical chemically to the water in another container, a conclusion is made that it is indeed one body. However, it is not true because the water in three containers is separated by the containers themselves. Therefore, water in three units does not equal one unit. A better view of that flawed argument of the Trinity can be seen in nature. When one bacterium undergoes mitosis, one says the result is two bacteria, not one organism separated by two complete membranes. Since mitosis does not end with the development of two organisms, a multitude of organisms ultimately arise, all genetically and physiologically identical (unless conjugation has occurred).

In terms of theology and spirits, the division of one spirit, in a manner similar to the mitosis of bacteria, into three spirits would produce a vast multitude of godlets, or little gods, from the original Lord God. It would basically be spiritual mitosis. Additionally, change can follow mitosis, such as in the case of stem cells. While stem cells can give rise to stem cells through mitosis, they can also develop further into different cells. An example is how a single fertilized oocyte can develop and produce stem cells, which in turn become cells which produce a multitude of tissues in the body. But, no one says that a neuron is identical to a skeletal muscle cell, even though they both originated from a single cell. Likewise, the concept of spiritual mitosis leaves the door open for development beyond the original division and the establishment of a polytheistic spiritual world. Yet, even that argument becomes flawed, since each spiritual being would have an origin and none would be eternal, omniscient, omnipotent, or omnipresent.

Even in the case where one approaches infinity, one can never be assured that one being would retain the same ranking in such a spiritual environment. What may be the top being one day could be far less in rank the next day. For the concept would emerge that in approaching infinity, one would have to consider the status at the onset of the growth, the relative ranking of beings (e.g., in terms of power, knowledge, wisdom) in time at the onset of growth, the increments of growth, and the rate of growth. So, what may be called the most powerful being in one particular day, because of differences in growth, would become less powerful in the next days. This would mean godhood itself would change from being to being. But, if a Being is indeed eternal, having no beginning, even the rate of growth would cease to be important. Why? Because no matter how far one can project into the future, one can still project indefinitely into the past. So, the emergence of gods succeeding gods becomes flawed and the presence of one God is sustained.

Approaching infinity does not mean that the nature of the contents, as indicated by the number set theory above, is all inclusive because the concept of incremental growth indicates that the growth is done in stages. Take for example two beings, represented by two sets of numbers. One increases by even numbers and approaches infinity. The other approaches infinity by odd numbers. While the first set may approach infinity, it would never include odd numbers. And, the second set would contain gaps (e.g., fractional values). Neither would contain such numbers as *pi* or the natural log. So, approaching infinity does not equate to becoming or being an infinite all-inclusive being. The gaps themselves would exclude the concepts of being omnipresent (since the gaps indicate lack of presence), omniscient (since the gaps represent lack of knowledge about something), or everlasting (since the gaps themselves indicate finiteness). As such, that which must grow can never become infinite, either in content or direction, and can never be God. And, anything finite can never become a god (or obtain godhood) since the limitations themselves indicate a structure that cannot approach true godhood. A true believer remains a child of the One and only God.

Having already presented the position that three containers actually represent three separate/ distinct beings (having delineations and independent compositions) and not one, another hypothesis has to be addressed. This hypothesis is that God the Father and God the Son are connected by a third Being or component, the Holy Spirit. The Holy Spirit then becomes just a force, not a God with His own identity/individuality. If that is the case, then there is no Trinity, but a two person Godhead. This argument, too, is erroneous. First, in being a force, the Holy Spirit can no longer have any emotion of His own. He could not grieve, for example. He would be unable to unite with Christ. He would not be able to dwell inside any believer. Instead, the Holy Spirit becomes merely an expression of power, but not of God. Second, in viewing the Holy Spirit as a joining factor, the Holy Spirit becomes synonymous to a bridge. That alone presents a problem in that it violates the concept of one set representing the nature of a single omnipotent, omnipresent, omniscient God. It would represent two identical sets combined by another set. Just as troubling, the bridge or uniting factor would lead to the assertion that some of the Godhead is more God than the rest of the Godhead. There arises the problem of God the Father being God and Christ being only a created Being and, therefore, not of the Godhead. Christ not being God is untrue.

From the standpoint of biology, when two persons are conjoined, the connecting tissue is not considered to be a separate entity. The two persons who are conjoined are viewed as being two separate individuals that have a common tissue bond. That tissue bond is not viewed as a single being. In such a case, the Holy Spirit, in comparison, would not be a Being (like the Father and the Son). Such would be in violation of a Trinity Godhead. Two beings joined together would violate the mathematical model already set forth. Thus, the concept that the Holy Spirit is merely a connective structure between God the Father and God the Son is false.

The fallacy of having two persons united by some connecting spirit can also be addressed by an analogy to chemistry. When two identical atoms combine to make a molecule, such as hydrogen or oxygen, the atoms are the same, but the bond between them is not called an atom. No, it is a result of the interaction of the identical atoms to form a molecule. Just as bonds do not become atoms, a connection between like persons does not mean that the connection becomes a person in and of itself. Doing so creates the problem that the bond, which is not the same as the two identical components, becomes in itself part of the unit without being the same as the component parts. Theologically speaking, if two beings, both spirit, needed a spirit to bind them, then the third spirit would not be the same as the two identical spirits. The consequence would not be a Trinity that comprises one God, three Beings (Father, Son, Holy Spirit) and one substance, but two persons and two substances. Or, one quickly develops a basis for polytheism in which some are greater gods than other gods. But, that would violate the principle established that only One Being is eternal, infinite, without beginning, and without ending. Moreover, from the standpoint of theology, if God is spirit, why would God need spirit to unify Himself? It would have all the logic of saying water needs water to be water or light needs light to be light.

Having the very nature that only God can possess (eternity [everlasting], omnipresence [all-present], omniscience [all-knowing], and omnipotence [all-powerful]), one can derive the answer to the question: "Can God ever do something that He cannot undo?" For example, can He build a rock so big that He could not move it? First of all, whatever he would do (God would construct) would have to have the characteristics of being eternal and omnipresent (or else one can simply go around it). But, those are reserved only for God. For God to do otherwise, would make whatever God constructed to become another god. Such would be imprudent. And, if God is anything, He is definitely not irrational or reckless. He is omniscient. Second, having the characteristics of eternity (everlasting), omnipresence (all-present), omniscience (all- knowing), and omnipotence (all-powerful), God has already decided on what He will do, when He will do it, where He will do it, and the consequences of doing it. God has the power to limit His power, but it is He who limits it, not another being or something else. And, even then, His power remains undiminished.

Having indicated that God alone has the characteristic

qualities of being complete (in wisdom, presence, knowledge, and power) at all times and in all places, how then can one say that God has created humanity in His image? Some would say that this indicates that we are gods in ourselves. But, a closer look at what was described before repudiates that. We are not in God's image because of the immensity of that which is contained in our nature. We are in God's image because of what can be done within our nature. Just as the complete number set indicated above is capable of having subsets and is able to perform mathematical operations t, so too can people change, adjust, create, and grow. They are much like smaller number sets capable of having and performing mathematical operations within the limits placed upon them by their very nature. But, as noted, none of those components or functions indicates godhood. It means God has permitted us to do things like Him, but that does not make us god or little gods. And, even if we endure into the eternal future, we can never become gods. The same holds true for all other beings with a beginning, including angels.

Knowing that only One can be eternal, omnipresent, omniscient, and omnipotent, only One can be God. And, as such, only One is worthy of worship as God.

Chapter Four: God: First in Love and First in Our Lives (God in Control)

Letting God take control of oneself is not a loss, but a gain. God does not want to be our Lord due to selfishness, but rather because of His love for us. After all, He sent His only begotten Son, into a world He so loved, so that those who believe in Him shall not perish, but have everlasting life. That means He acted to benefit others for their sakes, not because He was being selfish. And, His Son sacrificed Himself so that others could be forgiven of their sins and become sons and daughters of the One, eternal, living God.

God takes what we give Him, we sinful, impure beings. He cleanses us from sin and makes us pure in holiness. He heals those who had been sick. He puts life into those who had been dead. Then, He gives our lives back to us, so that we can be truly free and so that we can truly love Him. For love does not reside in slavery, but in being free. And love is not with the dead, but with the living. As such, God has not imposed upon us the law of subservience or abject submission, but the law that can only come from true love. He offers a gift of love unprecedented in all of history. And that love is the source of life.

God not only gives us life, but gives us the strength to live that life. He does not abandon us after having cured us. His cleansing is a spiritual vaccination so that we do not have to live under the dominance of sin and death. Even when trials and tribulations come upon us, they do not control us, for God's healing remains. And, God's healing remains because God is eternal, faithful and merciful.

So, what do we gain when we do not place our faith in God? We get to keep our sins. We remain unholy. Our illness remains. We stay dead, without life. As such, we gain nothing, but lose everything.

We cannot depend upon the belief that our good deeds make us worthy of heaven by offsetting the bad that we have done. There is no balance to decide between righteousness and unrighteousness to reward with life or death, respectively. The very concept of a judgmental balance is flawed for it assumes that good deeds wipe out evil deeds. The flaw becomes apparent in a simple balance between lives saved and lives taken. For instance, if one saves but one life more than one takes, one would be called righteous. But, if one takes one more life than one saves, one would be condemned. Another example would be in giving versus stealing. In terms of a balance equation, giving only a little more than stealing would make one righteous, while stealing a little more than giving would make one unrighteous. But, the fact is one would have to exercise judgment to decide who should live and who should die. Or, one would have to determine that what one stole versus that which one gave is of the same value to both the recipient and the victim. In order to do so, one would have to have perfect judgment and, consequently, place one's own judgment on an equal par with God's judgment. By focusing on one's own judgment, flawed as it is, one would then become one's own god, for one would have placed oneself into the center of one's attention/ focus. We become the balance by which we weigh our good and our bad. But, our balance is not God's measure of good versus evil. God sets His own standards. We are told to leave much to God. As a consequence, we are told neither to judge nor to seek vengeance. Both belong to God.

There is no other deity but God. That includes the fact that no one can supplant the judgment of God by one's own judgement (including our reportedly good deeds or thoughts). The belief that our good deeds make us worthy of heaven and of God means that one remains dead. For, in believing the aforementioned, we make ourselves equal unto God. But, God has warned us that there is none beside Him and His judgment is above all other judgments. Consequently, those who believe in their good deeds, rather than in God's good, have no resurrection unto life and remain dead. For, God will not give eternal life with Him unto those who seek to stand equal, in any way, unto Him. Moreover, such a belief also promotes the falsities that God can somehow be bribed by our good deeds or that somehow we are more righteous than God. If such a belief was true, God's blessings only become an economic transaction between the sinner and God. But, God cannot be bought by anyone, nor can His blessings be so obtained, for God is a respecter of no persons. In other words, God remains God over all persons. Just because we may revere ourselves above others does not mean that God does likewise. Additionally, by believing that we can somehow disregard what Christ has given to us via His death and resurrection, necessitating salvation based on our works and not on God's, means that we believe our righteousness is greater than the Lord's. And, that is simply blasphemy and idolatry. First, the false concept of obtaining salvation outside of Christ involves calling God a liar. Second, the idea that one must add to what Christ did for our salvation indicates that we must do something because the Lord did or could not. This would place us above the Lord. Yet, salvation comes from the Lord or it does not occur at all.

    We must have faith in the Lord and in what He has promised to us. We cannot let our past dictate our present or our future. The belief that one cannot be forgiven by the Lord not only denies the true power found in Christ's atoning sacrifice, but also indicates that one focuses only on oneself. If murder was unpardonable, then Paul would have never been an apostle of Christ. If fornication was unpardonable, then Solomon would have never been blessed. If adultery was unpardonable, then David would have never repented. And, if theft was unpardonable, then Matthew, a tax collector, would have never been a disciple of Christ. But, God did accept their repentance. He rewarded their faith in Him. As such, we must maintain our faith in God, for few sins are unpardonable. And those so mentioned specifically are blasphemy against the Holy Spirit and taking of the mark of the beast. So, as long as we breathe, we can repent and turn our faith, our focus, upon the Lord. For the blood of Christ is far more powerful than sin. And, God is far more powerful than we are. To avail ourselves of His wonderful mercy and saving grace, we must be willing to have faith in Him, turning away from our sins, denying even ourselves, losing our self-centered focus, letting God be the central focus of our lives, and walking in the way of His righteousness. This we must do while we live in this life. For this life will end. We cannot let the baggage of this life interfere with the happiness attainable in the next. And that means we must make God and His righteousness be the true focus of our lives.

We cannot depend upon the belief that we are basically good. For we actually have no basis for that belief. We reached such a conclusion due to our judgment and not due to the righteousness of God. As such, we overlook our sins and overemphasize what we perceive to be righteousness. Even if the heart is basically good, which is not, and deceives itself into so believing, that does not make the heart pure. Belief in one's purity does not make one pure. Believing that one is holy does not make one holy, regardless of how many would concur with such a conclusion. For such a belief has no standard. And, purity, being the complete absence of evil and sin, has to be measured against that which actually is completely good and sinless. In addition to being deceptive, the belief that one is basically good already, places the focus on oneself and removes the focus from God. When one does that, one is basically placing oneself in God's position, becoming a god unto oneself. But, there is no deity other than God. As such, we cannot place ourselves first or in place of God or in addition to God.

Knowing oneself does not assure righteousness. For, to know oneself, one needs to completely and honestly evaluate oneself. And, one must do so without any bias or deception. But how can the impure judge oneself who is no longer pure? How can one serve as one's own judge without becoming self-centered and self-serving upon oneself? To know oneself, the righteousness to be gained must be obtained from one who is far wiser and more righteous than us. That means our focus must again return to God who has that wisdom, righteousness, and love to do so. For God, not us, knows the destination that the path we are on will lead us. And knowing the path and the destination, He is the best teacher to guide us on how to overcome whatever obstacles we may face. As a consequence, to truly know ourselves, we must depend upon God. We must let God be our God. God has to be the center of our lives. We must let God do as He wills to us and our lives.

God does as God wills. Only God can restore the dead to life. And, He does so by His own judgment, His wisdom, His mercy, and His love. Only God can make that which had been enslaved by sin free from sin. And only God can give the strength to keep one free from sin's attempt to enslave us. Others may claim to have that power. But, they don't. For, they are only deceivers who are subservient to sin and who are spiritually dead unto true life. Just as death cannot give life, so too sin cannot purify. Those who are dead cannot make life. Those who are impure cannot make pure. But, that does not stop them from claiming that they can do so. For, sin is a liar and those who love sin are also liars.

God, in contrast, is truth. He is the true source of life. And, as such, He can give life to that which had been dead. And, God is infinitely holy. As such, He can purify those who had been ruled by sin. Because God is without any blemish, any impurity, and any sin, he is sterile to sin. And, God remains sterile to sin. Just like physical sterility can be compromised when contaminated with something not sterile, that which is sterile (from and of sin) cannot remain sterile (from and of sin) if it permits the unsterile (sin) to be part of it. As such, not even the smallest sin enters heaven. For, to do so, heaven would cease to be heaven. The pure would be made impure. Since sin is a disease, sin removes the health of and spreads malady among those who embrace it. If sin entered heaven, heaven would become another hell. As such, God cannot abide by any sin whatsoever in His presence. Truly, God makes sterile from sin those who believe. Only the sterile can make sterile. As such, only the holy can make holy. Only the wise can impart wisdom. And, only life can give life. The unholy can never make holy. Folly can never impart wisdom. The dead does not give life. The unclean cannot make clean, much less sterile. For nothing and no one can self-sterilize. Whosoever keeps his or her sin remains dead unto (spiritual) life. Whosoever serves another being besides God has no life from God.

In addition to being the source of life, God sustains life. And, God is all powerful. As such, He can give strength to those who have faith in Him to overcome any and all adversities, temptations, and trials.

Because real life comes from God, even the loss of this physical life does not mean that we lose the life from Him. God lives forever. God gives life. And, as such, He can make whosoever He wants to also live forever. So, when God asks for our lives, it is because He wants to give us true life, not to take it. For, God is no thief. He does not steal life for He is the true source of life. There is no other.

God is no tyrant. The choice to give our lives to Him or to cling to death is ours. If we want to be holy, He is the only one who can purify us. But, if we want to keep our sins, we keep our death. Nothing we can do by ourselves will purify us, free us from sin, or give us true life. No one but God can purify, free from sin, or give true life. So, if we want to remain impure, mastered by sin and death, we have only ourselves to blame. God will heal us and give us life, if only we let Him by giving ourselves completely unto Him.

What about the love for God and what does it do for the love of others? Actually, loving God first increases the love one has for another. The reason is that God is love. And, God being love, when He imparts Himself, leads to an increase in love. Does that mean one should focus one's life solely in prayer, in solitude from humankind, as an indication that one loves God? No, on the contrary, if all one does is pray, one is actually focused only on oneself. That is only a demonstration of self-love and an attempt to make God focus His love on that individual above any other. As such, it is not only selfish, but also an attempt to manipulate God (who cannot be manipulated or forced to do anything contrary to His nature or His will). To show that one actually loves God and is moved by God's love, one must let God express His love through the fruits of the Spirit that come from Him. The fruits of the Spirit are truly expressed in more than prayer. It is also expressed in rendering service to others, loving the truth, seeking wisdom, maintaining hope, being compassionate to others, and remaining faithful to God. As such, it is by loving God that we are healed, become whole, and also become capable of truly loving others. Loving God leads to loving others. And serving God leads to serving others.

The central focus of our lives must be God and we must love and serve Him first. Whatever is the primary focus of our lives rules our lives and becomes our de facto lord. If our purpose in life is to serve a cause, the cause becomes our lord and, therefore, our god. If our purpose is to serve country or any other institution or organization, that institution or organization becomes our lord and, therefore, our god. If our lives are centered by anyone other than God, then that other being becomes our lord. Those who we serve first are those who rule over us. Those who we love most are those who we serve most. If God is not first in our love, then we do not have God as our God, but have another in God's place. And, that is not acceptable to God.

There are people who claim that by serving them, one is actually serving God. Indeed, the world is full of detractors. There are multitudes who insist that we focus on their causes, desires, dreams, and beliefs. Many insist that we spend our lives learning their false paths or understanding, as well as accepting, their sins. There is no good fruit that comes from focusing on lies or sins. We ought to focus on God and His truth. This is to lead us in life and this is to be our life's central focus. As for the others, none of them can substitute for God. None of them can increase spiritual wisdom, grant salvation, or give life.

We cannot obtain from another being that which can only come from God. Life does not come from any other source. True love does not arise from another being. Salvation from sin cannot be obtained without God. As long as we remain centered on anything but God, as the true focus of our lives and our love, we miss out on so much and we suffer only loss. We have the choice to place our faith in God and His promises or to reject God and His promises. The former leads to life and more abundant love. The latter only leads to loneliness and destruction. The choice is ours and so are the rewards/consequences thereof.

In essence, we absolutely depend upon God. He gave us this life. His Word keeps us alive. And, He offers us the choice to have an even better/eternal life full of peace, joy, and love.

Chapter Five: Opposition to God and the Futility of Such Opposition

God is omnipotent, omniscient, and omnipresent. But, that does not mean that God is without opposition. However, no matter what anyone or anything does to oppose God, it ends up being an exercise in futility. As noted earlier in this book, anything or anyone with a beginning has only a finite capacity (e.g., power, knowledge, resources). That means no matter how much capacity one can acquire, develop, or influence, one can never become omnipotent, omniscient, or omnipresent. As a consequence, regardless of how much power one may have, this power is finite and will end. There is still an infinite amount of power that one does not have. No matter how much knowledge one may learn or master, this knowledge has a limit. There is still an infinite amount of knowledge one has not learned or mastered. And, no matter how far one may reach, this journey has a limit. There is an infinite realm beyond one's reach.

The earliest reported incidence of opposition to God came with the rebellion of angels who followed Lucifer in his quest to be equal to God. That attempt failed. God remained God and still has no equal. But, the opposition from that rebellion continues with humanity as the chess pieces being played. The deception that the fallen angels told themselves is still believed by much of humanity. The basic premise of the deception is rather simple. The deception is that there can be another deity besides God and, therefore, that other way can replace God's way. As a consequence, people consistently seek to find God in other deities, to serve God without having complete faith in Him, to have God change to meet their desires (e.g., accept them as His people and, consequently, accept their sins), and to replace spiritual worship with ritual.

Deception lies at the very heart of those who oppose God and would have others oppose Him. They believe that they will triumph simply because they either refuse to concede and/ or that God will have a change of heart regarding them. But, since God does not change, the latter won't happen. So, by refusing to concede, the ultimate objective is to hurt God. The objective is to cause as many as possible to reject God. That can only be done by deception. In contrast to many who proclaim that there are many forms of deception, there is only one real source of deception, namely those who originally opposed God. They would have people believe that there are many forms of deception in order to fragment the focus of persons who they would deceive. A fragmented or multifaceted deception appears more powerful than it really is and has the value of appealing to or threatening different persons. A sense of omnipresence of deception develops. But, that too is a deception. Only God is omnipresent. As such, deception is not omnipresent.

A multifaceted deception also appears to be more powerful than it really is. The deception may even appear to be irresistible and its success inevitable. One consequence of the feeling that the deception is more powerful than it really is that people lose hope in the truth. They become defeated and give up trying to truly follow God and have faith in Him. Another consequence is that believers become distracted from the mission given to them by the Lord. Rather than fighting the main fire of sin, believers spend their time chasing embers glowing in the sky which have been cast off by the principal fire. They lose sight of how to best serve God and also lose focus on God.

Those who oppose God can only do so temporarily. They do not have eternity to operate in. But, God, in contrast, does have eternity to do as He wills. Since that which is temporary has both a beginning and an ending, by definition it cannot prevail over that which has no beginning or ending. Eternity will always outlast the temporal. Additionally, the success of such opposition during its brief time is very limited. First, since those who oppose God are not omnipotent, they do not have the power sufficient to overcome the One who is omnipotent. In fact, they are actually powerless against God. Second, they cannot oppose God everywhere. They are not omnipresent. As such, even if they muster all their power at one particular point in time, at one locality, and with total focus, they would still be involved in a futile endeavor. Someone omnipotent (all-powerful) can always survive the power of anyone or everyone else, no matter how great their power may be. Omnipotence is always more powerful than limited power. Omnipresence is always where something limited to place cannot be. And omniscience never has to guess. But, that with limited knowledge often has to act without knowledge. Omniscience always outsmarts limited knowledge. So, because God is eternal, omnipotent, omnipresent, and omniscient, God can never be defeated or made to act contrary to His will.

That God cannot be made to change is fortunate. That means every promise He makes will be fulfilled. He gives life and the life He gives will be eternal. He truly blesses His people/ faithful believers. Because God is love, without any flaw, He can cleanse and make the impure pure. Since He does not change, He can, is to be and needs to be trusted. And, in that He is holy, He can and is to be loved. God is not only Lord, but a Lord worthy of our love, faith, lives, and dedication.

Chapter Six: Getting Closer to God

Christ informed us that God is Spirit and we must worship Him in spirit and truth. This means that physical efforts (works of the flesh), such as monetary measures and rituals, are not the way to worship the Lord God. So, what are the spiritual measures by which we should worship God? Paul (Gal. 5) informed us that the fruit of Spirit includes "love, joy, peace, patience, kindness, goodness, faithfulness, gentleness, and self-control." Taking that into account our worship of God should involve "love, joy, peace, patience, kindness, goodness, faithfulness, gentleness, and self-control." Moreover, since the fruits of the Spirit are involved in the worship of the Lord God, the Holy Spirit is intimately involved in such worship. For, the Holy Spirit transforms the Christian believer into becoming more Christ-like.

The Christian walk is a spiritual endeavor which has the Lord as not only the destination of the journey but also the journey itself. That Christ is the Way, the Spirit keeps one on the Way, and God the Father is the destination of the Way was addressed in an earlier chapter of this book. But, Christ did inform us that He is "the way, the truth and the life" and "no one goes unto the Father but through me." If one is to worship God in spirit and truth, then the fact that Jesus referred to Himself as the truth is important. It means one is to worship the Father in Him and by Him. That is one reason we were told to pray in Christ's name. Moreover, since Christ is the way, along with also being God, getting closer to God the Father involves Christ. In that no one goes to the Father but through Christ means that God the Son is the way unto God the Father; the Lord becomes the both the way and the destination. The importance of such was also addressed in an earlier chapter of this book.

Most people do not realize just how close God is already. Christ said He stands at the door, knocking on the unbeliever's heart, waiting to enter. Once Christ is within the believer, Christ, being God, not only gives us eternal life, but also cleanses us from sin which had separated us from God the Father. The Holy Spirit, also a Being of the Trinitarian Godhood, not only comforts us but also transforms us into becoming holy (pure from all sin) individuals who seek to do the will of God (Note: Some of this transformation into true holiness occurs after the resurrection of Christian believers into their spiritual bodies). One should note that this is all dependent upon faith, not through works. Works emerge because of the work of the Spirit upon us (such as bestowing of the fruits of the Holy Spirit). As such, one loves, just as God is love, because one of the fruits of the Holy Spirit is love. One has the peace of Christ, not in accordance with the peace of the world but, because one of the fruits of the Holy Spirit is peace. One does righteous works, not to prove that one is righteous or to gain salvation, but as a consequence of patience, kindness, and gentleness which are also fruits of the Holy Spirit. So, the Christian believer becomes more righteous not because of physical efforts, but because of spiritual transformation by the

Holy Spirit. And that spiritual transformation is the consequence of having placed one's faith in the Lord God through Christ the Lord.

The transformation also results in one seeking to be close with the Lord. His words in the Bible are sought diligently. His promises are believed wholeheartedly. And, one keeps seeking to live according to the way of the Lord, not because one seeks salvation from it, but because one finds pleasure in doing so and in glorifying the Lord. Moreover, because the Lord becomes such an integral part of one's life, one strives that the fruits of the Holy Spirit can be shared and enjoyed by others. The great commission of Christ to spread the good news worldwide and to all persons becomes not a burden (or even a means to salvation) but a privilege.

The truth is that there is a transformation which happens. Yet, many people actually fear undergoing such a change. They fear that they will lose their individuality and their freedom of choice. In actuality, the transformation enhances their uniqueness as persons. They lose their sins and gain their freedom. They gain their strength and decrease their weakness. They become the best person they can possibly be. And, they still retain their individuality. In contrast, those who do not become close to the Lord actually become enslaved (by sin and evil) and lose their distinct personalities. They become alike in their anger and hatred. They remain apart from God. They lose their individualities. They lose themselves in the process.

People often also claim to have faith in God, but do not live in accordance with that faith. This does not permit the Holy Spirit to truly transform the spirit of such persons. Consequently, they do not live close to God and are actually quite distant from Him. It is true that they may pray on occasion, often using the same words, but that does not have the impact of true prayer. For true prayer has a pivotal role in one's entire life. With prayer, one speaks to God as a truly beloved friend and Lord. As such, it is not based on the wording of the prayer or the act of praying to impress everyone but it is intimate, personal and a deep interaction between two spirits. Prayer is not always a pleading for something or for deliverance from something. Prayer represents an ongoing celebration of the closeness that one has with the Lord. And, because of that communication, one becomes increasingly close to God and increasingly more aware of the love that God has one. No one can be intimate with God without becoming closer to God. And, no one can become close to God without living according to the will of God. As such, the first step is faith in believing Christ and letting Him be one's Lord. The second step is to allow the Holy Spirit to transform one into a truly righteous individual. The third step, along with doing what the Lord has told one to do (because of the transforming power of the Holy Spirit), is to develop and nurture a truly loving and open relationship with the Lord God (for example, with true prayer). The closer that one becomes with the Lord opens the door to an even closer relationship. The Lord God becomes not only our Lord, but our perfect parent. That relationship is not just in and for this lifetime. It is for all eternity.

Appendix: Important Bible Passages Regarding God (King James Version)

Christ (God the Son)

His name shall be called Wonderful, Counsellor, The mighty God, The everlasting Father, The Prince of Peace (Isa. 9:6).

Behold, one like the Son of man came with the clouds of heaven, and came to the Ancient of days, and they brought Him near before Him. And there was given Him dominion, and glory, and a Kingdom, that all people, nations, and languages, should serve Him: His dominion is an everlasting dominion, which shall not pass away, and His Kingdom that which shall not be destroyed (Dan. 7:12, 14).

Behold a virgin shall be with child, and shall bring forth a son, and they shall call His name Emmanuel, which being interpreted is, God with us (Matt. 1:23; Isa. 7:14).

Lo a voice from heaven, saying, This is my beloved Son, in whom I am well pleased (Matt. 3:17; Mark 1:11; Luke 3:22).

While He yet spake, behold a bright cloud overshadowed them: and behold a voice out of the cloud, which said, This is My beloved Son, in whom I am well pleased; hear ye Him (Matt. 17:5; Mark 9:7; Luke 9:35).

For where two or three are gathered together in My name, there am I in the midst of them (Matt. 18:20).

And Jesus came and spake unto them, saying, All power is given unto Me in heaven and in earth (Matt. 28:18).

I am with you always, even unto the end of the world (Matt. 28:20).

Again the high priest asked Him, and said unto Him, Art Thou the Christ, the Son of the Blessed? And Jesus said, I am: and ye shall see the Son of man sitting on the right hand of power, and coming in the clouds of heaven (Mark 14:61).

All things are delivered to Me of My Father: and no man knoweth who the Son is, but the Father; and who the Father is, but the Son, and he to whom the Son will reveal Him (Luke 10:22).

In the beginning was the Word, and the Word was with God, and the Word was God, The same was in the beginning with God (John 1:1, 2).

The Word was made flesh, and dwelt among us (and we beheld His glory, the glory as of the only begotten of the Father,) full of grace and truth (John 1:14).

All men should honour the Son, even as they honour the Father. He that honoureth not the Son honoureth not the Father which hath sent Him (John 5:23).

My judgment is just; because I seek not mine own will, but the will of the Father which hath sent Me (John 5:30).

I came down from heaven, not to do Mine own will, but the will of Him that sent me (John 6:38).

I am the living bread which came down from heaven; if any man eat of this bread, he shall live forever: and the bread that I will give is My flesh, which I will give for the life of the world (John 6:51).

Jesus answered them, and said, My doctrine is not Mine, but His that sent Me (John 7:16).

I am the light of the world, he that followeth Me shall not walk in darkness, but shall have the light of life (John 8:12).

Jesus ... said unto him, Dost thou believe on the Son of God? He answered and said, Who is He, Lord, that I might believe on Him? Jesus said unto him, Thou hast both seen him, and it is He that talketh with thee (John 9:35).

I and My Father are one (John 10:30).

He that seeth Me seeth Him that sent Me (John 12:45).

Jesus knowing that the Father had given all things into His hands, and that He was come from God, and went to God (John 13:3).

Ye call Me Master and Lord: and ye say well; for so I am (John 13:13).

I am the way, the truth, and the life: no man cometh unto the Father, but by Me (John 14:6).

He that hath seen Me hath seen the Father (John 14:9).

I go my way to Him that sent Me. All things that the Father hath are Mine. The Father Himself loveth you, because you have loved Me, and have believed that I came out from God. I came forth from the Father, and am come into the world: again, I leave the world, and go to the Father, I am not alone, because the Father is with Me (John 16: 5, 15, 27, 28, 32).

But these are written, that ye might believe that Jesus is the Christ, the Son of God, and that believing ye might have life through His name (John 20:31).

Him hath God exalted with His right hand to be a Prince and a Saviour, for to give repentance to Israel, and forgiveness of sins (Acts 5:31).

He hath commanded us to preach unto the people, and to testify that it is He which was ordained of God to be the Judge of the quick and dead (Acts 10:42).

The gift of God is eternal life through Jesus Christ our Lord (Rom. 6:23).

To this end Christ both died, and rose, and revived, that He might be Lord both of the dead and living (Rom. 14:9).

We shall all stand before the judgment seat of Christ (Rom. 14:10).

Now He that hath wrought us for the selfsame thing is God, who also hath given unto us the earnest of the Spirit. All things are of God (2 Cor. 5:5).

We must all appear before the judgment seat of Christ; that every one may receive the things done in his body, according to that he hath done, whether it be good or bad (2 Cor. 5:10).

Christ sitteth on the right hand of God (Col. 3:1).

There is one God, and one mediator between God and men, the man Christ Jesus (1 Tim. 2:5).

If we suffer, we shall also reign with Him: if we deny Him, He also will deny us (2 Tim. 2:12).

Jesus Christ the same yesterday, and today, and forever (Heb. 13:8).

Who is a liar but he that denieth that Jesus is the Christ? He is antichrist, that denieth the Father and the Son. Whosoever denieth the Son, the same hath not the Father (1 John 2: 22, 23).

I am Alpha and Omega, the beginning and the ending, saith the Lord, which is, and which was, and which is to come, the Almighty. I am Alpha and Omega, the first and the last: I am the first and the last: I am He that liveth, and was dead (Rev. 1:8, 11, 17, 18).

He hath on His vesture and on His thigh a name written, King of Kings, and Lord of Lords (Rev. 19:16).

Creator

In the beginning God created the heaven and the earth (Gen. 1:1).

God said, Let us make man in our image, after our likeness. So God created man in His own image, in the image of God created He him; male and female created He them (Gen. 1:26, 27).

The Lord made heaven and earth, the sea, and all that in them (Psa. 146:6).

All the gods of the people are idols; but the Lord made the heavens (1 Chr. 16:26).

The day is Thine, the night also is Thine: Thou hast prepared the light and the sun. Thou has set all the borders of the earth; Thou hast made summer and winter (Psa. 72:16, 17).

The heavens are Thine, the earth also is Thine: as for the world and the fullness thereof, thou hast founded them (Psa. 89:11).

Our help is in the name of the Lord, which made heaven and earth (Psa. 124:8).

To Him that by wisdom made the heavens: to Him that stretched out the earth above the waters: To Him that made the great lights: The Sun to rule by day: The moon and stars to rule by night (Psa. 136:5-9).

The Lord hath made all things for Himself (Prov. 16:4).

I form the light, and create darkness: I make peace, and create evil: I the Lord do all these things. I have made the earth, and created man upon it: I even my hands, have stretched out the heavens, and all their host have I commanded. Thus saith the Lord that created the heavens: God Himself that formed the earth and made it; He hath established it, He created it not in vain, He formed it to be inhabited (Isa. 45:7, 12, 18).

Mine hand also hath laid the foundation of the earth, and my right hand hath spanned the heavens: when I call unto them, they stand up together (Isa. 48:13).

I have made the earth, the man and the beast that are upon the ground (Jer. 27:5).

From the beginning of the creation God made them [humanity] male and female (Mark 10:6).

God that made the world and all things therein (Acts 17:24).

The fellowship of the mystery, which from the beginning of the world hath been hid in God, who created all things by Jesus Christ (Eph. 3:9).

By Him [Christ] were all things created, that are in heaven, and that are in earth, visible and invisible, whether they be thrones, or dominions, or principalities, or powers; all things were created by Him, and for Him: and He is before all things, and by Him all things consist (Col. 1:16).

Thou art worthy, O Lord, to receive glory and honour and power: for thou hast created all things, and for Thy pleasure they are and were created (Rev. 10: 6).

Everlasting (Eternal)

I lift my hand to heaven, and say, I live forever (Deut. 32:40).

The eternal God is thy refuge, and underneath are the everlasting arms (Deut. 33:27).

The Lord shall endure forever (Psa. 9:7).

The glory of the Lord shall endure forever (Psa. 104:31).

His righteousness endureth forever (Psa. 111:3).

The high and lofty One that inhabiteth eternity (Isa. 57:15).

Your name is from everlasting (Isa. 63:16).

Who only hath immortality, dwelling in the light which no man can approach unto; whom no man hath seen, nor can see (1 Tim. 6:16).

One day is with the Lord as a thousand years, and a thousand years as one day (2 Pet. 3: 8). Him that liveth forever and ever, Who created heaven, and the things that therein are, and the sea, and the things which are therein (Rev. 10:6).

Faithfulness of

The word of the Lord is right; and all His works are done in truth (Psa. 33:4).

His truth endureth to all generations (Psa. 100:5).

The truth of the Lord endureth forever (Psa. 117:2).

Great is Thy faithfulness (Lam. 3:23).

He that sent Me is true (John 8:26).

God is faithful, by Whom ye were called unto the fellowship of His Son Jesus Christ, our Lord (1 Cor. 1:9).

God is faithful, Who will not suffer you to be tempted above that ye are able (1 Cor. 1:13).

Faithful is He that calleth you, who also will do it (1 Thess. 5:24).

The Lord is faithful, who shall establish you, and keep you from evil (2 Thess. 3:3).

If we believe not, yet He abideth faithful: He cannot deny Himself. The foundation of God standeth sure, having this seal, The Lord knoweth them that are His (2 Tim. 2:13, 19).

The Lord is not slack concerning His promise, as some men count slackness (2 Pet. 3:9).

If we confess our sins, He is faithful and just to forgive us our sins, and to cleanse us from all unrighteousness (1 John 1:9).

Glory of

The heavens declare the glory of God; and the firmament sheweth His handywork (Psa. 191:1).

The glory of the Lord shall endure forever: the Lord shall rejoice in His works (Psa. 104:31).

The Lord is high above all nations, and His glory above the heavens (Psa. 113:4).

Holy, holy, holy, is the Lord of hosts: the whole earth is full of His glory (Isa. 6:3).

As the heavens are higher than the earth, so are My ways higher than your ways, and My thoughts than your thoughts (Isa. 55:9).

Godhead (Trinity)

God said, Let is make man in our image, after our likeness (Gen. 1:26).

And he Lord God said, Behold, the man is become as one of Us, to know good and evil (Gen. 3:22).

And one cried unto another, and said, Holy, holy, holy, is the Lord of hosts: the whole earth is full of His glory. Also I heard the voice of the Lord, saying, Whom shall I send, and who will go for Us? (Isa. 6:3).

Come ye near unto Me, hear ye this; I have not spoken in secret from the beginning; from the time that it was, there am I: and now the Lord God, and His Spirit, hath sent me (Isa. 48:16).

Jesus, when He was baptized, went straightway out of the water; and lo, the heavens were opened unto Him, and He saw the Spirit of God descending like a dove, and lighting upon Him, And lo a voice from heaven, saying, This is My beloved Son, in whom I am well pleased (Mark 1:10; Luke 3:22; John 1:32).

Go ye therefore, and teach all nations, baptizing them in the name of the Father, and of the Son, and of the Holy Ghost [Spirit] (Matt. 28:19).

For David himself said by the Holy Ghost, The Lord said to my Lord, Sit Thou on My right hand, till I make Thine enemies Thy footstool (Mark 12:36).

The angel answered and said unto her, The Holy Ghost shall come upon thee, and the power of the Highest shall overshadow thee; therefore also that holy thing which shall be born of thee shall be called the Son of God (Luke 1:35).

Jesus being full of the Holy Ghost returned from Jordan, and was led by the Spirit into the wilderness, Jesus returned in the power of the Spirit into Galilee (Luke 4:1, 14).

I will pray the Father, and He shall give you another Comforter, that he may abide with you forever. Even the Spirit of Truth; whom the world cannot receive, because it seeth Him not, neither knoweth Him: but ye know Him; for He dwelleth with you, and shall be in you. But the Comforter, which is the Holy Ghost, whom the Father will send in My name, he shall teach you all things, and bring all things to your remembrance, whatsoever I have said unto you (John 14:16, 17, 26).

When the Comforter is come, whom I will send unto you from the Father, even the Spirit of Truth, which proceedeth from the Father, he shall testify of Me (John 15:26).

To us there is but one God, the Father, of Whom are all things, and we in Him; and one Lord Jesus Christ, by Whom are all things, and we by Him (1 Cor. 8:6).

Guide

Thus saith the Lord, thy Redeemer, the Holy One of Israel; I am the Lord thy God which teacheth thee to profit, which leadeth thee by the way that thou shouldest go (Isa. 48:17).

And the Lord shall guide thee continually, and satisfy thy soul in drought, and make fat thy bones: and thou shalt be like a watered garden, and like a spring of water, whose waters fail not (Isa. 58:11).

Holiness

I the Lord your God am holy (Lev. 19:2).

There is none holy as the Lord (1 Sam. 2:2).

As for God, His way is perfect (Psa. 18:30).

God sitteth upon the throne of His holiness (Psa. 47:8).

God hath spoken in His holiness (Psa. 60:6).

Holy and reverent is His name (Psa. 111:9).

There is no iniquity with the Lord our God, nor respect of persons, not taking of gifts (2 Chr. 19:7).

The high and lofty One that inhabiteth eternity, whose name is Holy (Isa. 57:15).

Be ye therefore perfect, even as your Father which is in heaven is perfect (Matt. 5:48).

There is none good but one, that is, God (Matt. 19:17).

Holy is His name (Luke 1:49).

God cannot be tempted with evil, neither tempteth He any man (Jas. 1:13).

God is light, and in Him is no darkness at all (1 John 1:5).

Holy, holy, holy, Lord God Almighty, which was, and is, and is to come (Rev. 4:8).

Who shall not fear thee, O Lord, and glorify Thy name? For Thou only art holy (Rev. 15:4).

Holy Spirit (Holy Ghost)

[Jesus said] I cast out devils by the Spirit of God (Matt. 19:28).

Jesus answered, Verily, verily, I say unto thee, Except a man be born of water and of the Spirit, he cannot enter into the Kingdom of God. That which is born of the flesh is flesh; and that which is born of the Spirit is spirit. For He whom God hath sent speaketh the words of God: for God giveth not the Spirit by measure unto Him (John 3:5, 6, 34).

Nevertheless, I tell you the truth; It is expedient for you that I go away: for if I go not away, the Comforter will not come unto you; but if I depart, I will send Him unto you. And when He is come, He will reprove the world of sin, and of righteousness, and of judgment: Of sin, because they believe not on Me; Of righteousness, because I go to my Father, and ye see me no more; Of judgment, because the prince of this world is judged. I have yet many things to say unto you, but ye cannot bear them now. Howbeit when He, the Spirit of Truth, is come, He will guide you into all truth: for He shall not speak of Himself; but whatsoever He shall hear, that shall He speak: and He will shew you things to come. He shall glorify Me: for He shall receive of Mine, and shall shew it unto you (John 16:7-14).

The love of God is shed abroad in our hearts by the Holy Ghost which is given unto us (Rom. 5:5).

The Kingdom of God is not meat and drink; but righteousness, and peace, and joy in the Holy Ghost (Rom. 14:17).

We speak, not in the words which man's wisdom teacheth, but which the Holy Ghost teacheth; comparing spiritual things with spiritual (1 Cor. 2:13).

Know ye not that ye are the temple of God, and that the Spirit of God dwelleth in you? (1 Cor. 3:16).

Wherefore I give you to understand, that no man speaking by the Spirit of God calleth Jesus accursed: and that no man can say that Jesus is the Lord, but by the Holy Ghost. Now there are diversities of gifts, but the same Spirit. And there are differences of administrations, but the same Lord. And there are diversities of operations, but it is the same God which worketh all in all. But the manifestation of the Spirit is given to everyman to profit withal. For to one is given by the Spirit the word of wisdom; To another the word of knowledge by the same Spirit; To another faith by the same Spirit; to another the gifts of healing by the same Spirit; To another the working of miracles; To another prophecy; To another discerning of spirits; To another diverse kinds of tongues; To another the interpretation of tongues: But all these worketh that one and the selfsame Spirit, dividing to every man severally as He will (1 Cor. 3-11).

Where the Spirit of the Lord is, there is liberty. But we all, with open face beholding as in a glass the glory of the Lord, are changed into the same image from glory to glory, even as by the Spirit of the Lord (2 Cor. 3:17, 18).

Received ye the Spirit by the works of law, or by the hearing of faith? Are ye so foolish: having begun in the Spirit, are ye now made perfect by the flesh? That we might receive the promise of the Spirit through faith (Gal. 3:2, 3, 14).

Because ye are sons, God hath sent forth the Spirit of His Son into your hearts, crying, Abba, Father (Gal. 4:6).

We through the Spirit wait for the hope of righteousness by faith. Walk in the Spirit, and ye shall not fulfil the lust of the flesh. For the flesh lusteth against the Spirit, and the Spirit against the flesh: and these are contrary the one to the other: so that ye cannot do the things that ye would. But, if ye be led of the Spirit, ye are not under the law. But, the fruit of the Spirit is love, joy, peace, long-suffering, gentleness, goodness, faith, meekness, temperance: against such there is no law. If we live in the Spirit, let us also walk in the Spirit (Gal. 5:5, 16-18, 22, 23, 25).

He that soweth to the Spirit shall of the Spirit reap life everlasting (Gal. 6:8).

Hereby we now that He abideth in us, by the Spirit which He hath given us (1 John 3:24).

Jealous

I the Lord thy God am a jealous God. The Lord will not hold him guiltless that taketh His name in vain (Deut. 5:9, 11).

The Lord thy God is a consuming fire, even a jealous God (Deut. 4:24).

Judge

For the Lord your God is God of gods, and Lord of lords, a great God, a mighty and a terrible, which regardeth not persons, nor taketh rewards (Deut. 10:17).

He is the Rock, His work is perfect: for all His ways are judgment: a God of truth and without iniquity, just and right is He. To Me belongeth vengeance, and recompense (Duet 32:4, 35).

The adversaries of the Lord shall be broken to pieces; out of heaven shall He thunder upon them: the Lord shall judge the ends of the earth (1 Sam. 2:10).

Then shall the trees of the wood sing out at the presence of the Lord, because He cometh to judge the earth (1 Chr. 16:33).

The righteous God trieth the heart and reins. God judgeth the righteous, and God is angry with the wicked every day (Psa. 7 9, 11).

The judgments of the Lord are true and righteous altogether (Psa. 19:9).

He loveth righteousness and judgment (Psa. 33:5).

Verily there is a reward for the righteous: verily He is a God that judgeth the earth (Psa. 58:11).

Thou renderest to every man according to his work (Psa. 62:12).

Justice and judgment are the habitation of Thy throne: mercy and truth shall go before Thy face (Psa. 89:14).

The Lord executeth righteousness and judgement for all that are oppressed (Psa. 103:6).

All the ways of man are clean in his own eyes; but the Lord weigheth the spirits (Prov. 16:2).

Every ways of a man is right in his own eyes: but the Lord pondereth the hearts. To do justice and judgment is more acceptable to the Lord than sacrifice (Prov. 21:2, 3).

Every man's judgment cometh from the Lord (Prov. 29:26).

God shall bring every work into judgment, with every secret thing, whether it be good, or whether it be evil (Eccl. 12:14).

For the Lord is our judge, the Lord is our lawgiver, the Lord is our King; He will save us (Isa. 33:22).

I the Lord love judgment, I hate robbery for burnt offering (Isa.61:8).

I am the Lord which exercise loving kindness, judgment, and righteousness, in the earth: for in these things I delight, saith the Lord (Jer. 9:24).

The Lord is slow to anger, and great in power, and will not at all acquit the wicked (Nah. 1:3).

Fear Him which is able to destroy both soul and body in hell (Matt. 10:28).

Who will render to every man according to his deeds: For there is no respect of persons with God (Rom. 2:6).

Knowing that whatsoever good thing any man doeth, the same shall he receive of the Lord (Eph. 6:8).

He hath appointed a day, in which He will judge the world in righteousness by that man whom He hath ordained (Acts 17:31).

The Father, Who without respect of persons judgeth according to every man's work (1 Pet. 1:17).

True and righteous are His judgments (Rev. 19:2).

Love of

Fear thou not; for I am with thee: be not dismayed; for I am God (Isa. 41:10).

God is love (1 John 4:8).

Mercy of

The Lord your God is gracious and merciful, and will not turn away His face from you, if ye return unto Him (2 Chr. 30:9).

The mercy of the Lord is from everlasting to everlasting upon them that fear Him, and His righteousness unto children's children (Psa. 103:17).

O give thanks unto the Lord; for He is good: for His mercy endureth forever (Psa. 118:29).

They shall abundantly utter the memory of Thy great goodness. The Lord is good to all: and His tender mercies are all over all His works (Psa. 145:7).

He is kind unto the unthankful and to the evil (Luke 6:35).

Omnipotent (All-powerful)

I kill, and I make alive; I wound, and I heal: neither is there any that can deliver out of My hand (Deut. 32:39).

The Lord killeth, and maketh alive: He bringeth down to the grave, and bringeth up. The Lord maketh poor, and maketh rich: He bringeth low, and lifteth up (1 Sam. 2:6, 7).

There is no restraint to the Lord, to save by many or by few (1 Sam. 14:6).

He spake, and it was done; He commanded, and it stood fast (Psa. 33:9).

Whatsoever the Lord pleased, that did He in heaven, and in earth, in the seas, and all deep places (Psa. 135:6).

He commanded, and they were created (Psa. 248:5).

Surely as I have thought, so shall it come to pass; and as I have purposed, so shall it stand: The Lord of hosts hath purposed, and who shall disannul it? and His hand is stretched out, and who shall turn it back? (Isa. 14:24, 27).

In the Lord Jehovah is everlasting strength (Isa. 26:4).

There is none that can deliver out of My hand (Isa. 43:13).

My counsel shall stand, and I do all My pleasure: I have spoken it, I will also bring it to pass; I have purposed it, I will also do it (Isa. 46:10, 11).

The Lord's hand is not shortened, that it cannot save; neither His ear heavy, that it cannot hear (Isa. 59:1).

He doeth according to His will in the army of heaven, and among the inhabitants of the earth: and none can stay His hand, or say unto Him, What doest Thou? (Dan. 4:35).

With God all things are possible (Matt. 19:26).

Father, all things are possible unto thee (Mark 14:36).

With God nothing shall be impossible (Luke 1:37).

What He had promised, He was able also to perform (Rom. 4:21).

God hath both raised up the Lord, and will also raise up us by His own power (1 Cor. 6:14).

Omnipresent (All-Present)

Am I a God at hand, saith the Lord, and not a God afar off? Can any hide himself in secret places that I shall not see him? saith the Lord. Do not I fill heaven and earth? saith the Lord (Jer. 23:23, 24).

The eyes of the Lord are in every place, beholding the evil and the good (Prov. 5:21).

Omniscient (All-Knowing)

The Lord is a God of knowledge, and by Him actions are weighed (1 Sam. 2:3).

The Lord seeth not as man seeth; for man looketh on the outward appearance, but the Lord looketh on the heart. The Lord searcheth all hearts, and understandeth all the imaginations of the thoughts (1 Chr. 28:9).

Great is our Lord, and of great power: His understanding is infinite (Psa. 147:5).

God knoweth your hearts (Luke 16:15).

Opposition To

There is no wisdom nor understanding nor counsel against the Lord (Prov. 21:30).

Parenthood

Call no man your father on earth: for one is your Father, which is in heaven (Matt, 23:9).

Behold, what manner of love the Father hath bestowed upon us, that we should be called the sons of God (1 John 3:1).

Righteousness of

The righteous Lord loveth righteousness; His countenance doth behold the upright (Psa. 11:7).

Good and upright is the Lord (Psa. 25:8).

The earth is full of the goodness of the Lord (Psa. 33:5).

O taste and see that the Lord is good (Psa. 34:8).

There is no unrighteousness in Him (Psa. 92:15).

The Lord is good; His mercy is everlasting (Psa. 100:5).

O give thanks unto the Lord; for He is good (Psa. 106.1).

The earth, O Lord, is full of Thy mercy: Thou art good, and doest good (Psa. 119:64, 68).

The Lord is righteous (Psa. 129:4).

The Lord is righteous in all His ways, and holy in all His works (Psa. 145:17).

I the Lord speak righteousness, I declare things that are right (Isa. 45:19).

I am the Lord which exercise loving kindness, judgment, and righteousness, in the earth: for in these things I delight, saith the Lord (Jer. 9:24).

The Lord is good unto them that wait for Him, to the soul that seeketh Him (Lam. 3:25).

The just Lord is in the midst thereof; He will not do iniquity: every morning doth He bring His judgment to light, He faileth not (Zeph. 3:5).

Is there unrighteousness with God? God forbid (Rom. 9:14).

Just and true are Thy ways, Thou King of saints (Rev. 15:3).

Ruler

The Lord your God is God of gods, and Lord of lords, a great God, a mighty, and a terrible (Deut. 10:17).

The earth is the Lord's, and the fullness thereof, and they that dwell therein (Psa. 24:1).

Thy Kingdom is an everlasting kingdom, and Thy dominion endureth throughout all generations (Psa. 145:13).

The Lord shall reign forever, even thy God, O Zion, unto all generations (Psa. 146:10).

Is He the God of the Jews only? is He not also of the Gentiles? Yes, of the Gentiles also (Rom. 3:29).

Savior

I will dwell in the house of the Lord forever (Psa. 23:6).

Call upon Me in the day of trouble: I will deliver thee, and thou shalt glorify Me (Psa. 50:15).

Thou shalt know no god but Me: for there is no saviour beside me (Hos. 24:4).

God so loved the world, that He gave His only begotten Son, that whosoever believeth in Him should not perish, but have everlasting life (John 3:16).

We know that all things work together for good for them that love God (Rom. 8:28).

Eye hath not seen, nor ear heard, neither have entered into the heart of man, the things which God hath prepared for them that love Him (1 Cor. 2:9).

You are the temple of the living God; as God hath said, I will dwell in them, and walk in them; and I will be their God, and they shall be My people (2 Cor. 6:16).

The Lord knoweth how to deliver the godly out of temptations, and to reserve the unjust unto the day of judgment to be punished (2 Pet. 2:9).

If we confess our sins, He is faithful and just to forgive us our sins, and to cleanse us from all unrighteousness (1 John 1:9).

Trustworthy

How excellent is Thy loving kindness, O God! Therefore the children of men put their trust under the shadow of Thy wings (Psa. 36:7).

Truth of

Howbeit when He, the Spirit of Truth, is come, He will guide you into all truth (John 10:3).

In hope of eternal life, which God, that cannot lie, promised before the world began (Tit. 1:2).

Unchangeable (Immutable)

God is not a man, that He should lie; neither the Son of man, that He should repent: heath He said, and shall He not do it? Behold I have received and commend it good? Behold, I have received commandment to bless, and He hath blessed; and I cannot reverse it (Num. 23: 19, 20).

The counsel of the Lord standeth forever, the thoughts of His heart to all generations (Psa. 33:11).

Whatsoever God doeth, it shall be forever: nothing can be put to it, nor anything taken from it (Eccl. 3:14).

He also is wise, and will bring evil, and will not call back His words (Isa. 31:2).

Hast thou not heart, that the everlasting God, the Lord, the Creator of the ends of the earth, fainteth not, neither is weary? (Isa. 40:28).

I am the Lord, I change not (Mal. 3:6).

Every good gift and every perfect gift is from above, and cometh down from the Father of lights, with Whom there is no variableness, neither shadow of turning (Jas. 1:7).

Uniqueness of

That thou mayest know that there is none like unto the Lord our God (Ex. 8:10).

Thou shalt have no other gods before Me (Ex. 20:3).

Hear, O Israel: The Lord our God is one Lord (Deut. 6:4).

The Lord He is God; there is none else beside Him. The Lord He is God in heaven above, and upon the earth beneath: there is none else (Deut. 4:35, 39).

There is none holy as the Lord: for there is none beside Thee: neither is there any rock like our God (1 Sam. 2:2).

There is none like Thee, neither is there any God beside Thee (2 Sam. 7:22).

There is no God like Thee, in heaven above, or on earth beneath, That all the people of the earth may know that the Lord is God, and that there is none else (1 Kin. 8:23, 60).

Thou art the God, even thou alone, of all the kingdoms of the earth; thou hast made heaven and earth (2 Kin. 19:15).

Thou, even thou, art Lord alone; ... and the host of heaven worshippeth thee (Neh. 9:6).

I am the Lord: that is my name: and My glory will I not give another, neither my praise to graven images (Isa. 42:8).

I am He: before Me there was no God formed, neither shall there be after Me. I, even I, am the Lord, and beside Me there is no saviour (Isa. 43:10, 11).

I am the first, and I am the last; and beside Me there is no God. Is there a God beside Me? yea, there is no God; I know not any (Isa. 44:6, 8).

I am the Lord, and there is none else, there is no God beside me: That they may know from the rising of the sun, and from the west, that there is none beside Me. I am the Lord, and there is none else. There is no God beside me; a just God and a Saviour; there is none beside Me (Isa. 45:5, 6, 21).

To whom will ye liken Me, and make Me equal, and compare Me, that we may be like? I am God, and there is none else; I am God, and there is none like Me (Isa. 46:5, 9).

There is no God else beside Me: a just God and a Saviour (Isa. 45:21).

I am God, and there is none like me (Isa. 46:9).

Now unto the King eternal, immortal, invisible, the only wise God, be honour and glory forever and ever (1 Tim. 6:16).

Vengeful

God is jealous, and the Lord revengeth; the Lord revengeth, and is furious; the Lord will take vengeance on His adversaries (Nah. 1:2).

Worshipping of

Him shall ye fear, and Him shall ye worship, and to Him shall ye do sacrifice (2 Kin. 17:36).

Thou shalt worship the Lord thy God, and Him only shalt thou serve (Matt. 4:10).

www.ingramcontent.com/pod-product-compliance
Lightning Source LLC
Chambersburg PA
CBHW052105070526
44584CB00017B/2344